The Transition Metals 2

Gold, Iron and Other Elements

THE PERIODIC TABLE

Nigel Saunders

Heinemann

www.heinemann.co.uk/library

Visit our website to find out more information about Heinemann Library books.

To order:

 Phone 44 (0) 1865 888066

 Send a fax to 44 (0) 1865 314091

Visit the Heinemann Bookshop at www.heinemann.co.uk/library to browse our catalogue and order online.

First published in Great Britain by Heinemann Library, Halley Court, Jordan Hill, Oxford OX2 8EJ, part of Harcourt Education. Heinemann is a registered trademark of Harcourt Education Ltd.

Editorial: Sarah Eason and Kathy Peltan
Design: David Poole and
    Tinstar Design Limited (www.tinstar.co.uk)
Illustrations: Geoff Ward and Paul Fellows
Picture Research: Rosie Garai
Production: Viv Hichens
Originated by Blenheim Colour Ltd
Printed and bound in Hong Kong and China
    by South China

ISBN 0 431 16980 2
08 07 06 05 04
10 9 8 7 6 5 4 3 2 1

British Library Cataloguing in Publication Data
Saunders, Nigel
   The transition metals: Gold, iron and other metals. – (The periodic table)
   546.6
A full catalogue record for this book is available from the British Library.

Acknowledgements

The publishers would like to thank the following for permission to reproduce photographs:

Action Plus p25; Ancient Art & Architecture p23; Corbis pp4, 16 (James L Amos), 21 (Kevin R Morris), 27 (Royal Ontario Museum), 31, 39 (Chris Collins), 41 top (Stapleton Collection), 42, 43 (Roger Garwood & Trish Ainslie), 57 (Michael S Yamashita); Diy Photo Library p37; Photodisc pp24, 35, 48; Rolls Royce p52; Science Photo Library pp11 (Astrid & Hans-Frieder Michler), 13 (BSIP, SERCOM), 15 (D Van Ravenswaay), 18 (David Parker), 20 (Sinclair Stammers), 26 (Russ Lappa), 30 (Klaus Guldbrandsen), 33 (Science Museum), 34 (Kaj R Svensson), 38 (Pascal Goetgheluck), 44 (NASA), 46, 50, 51 (Russ Lappa), 54 (Alfred Pasieka); Trevor Clifford pp29, 32, 40 (bottom), 47; Tudor Photography pp53, 55; Zefa p49 (rud-gr.com).

Cover photograph of gold bars and nuggets reproduced with permission of Getty Images.

The author would like to thank Angela, Kathryn, David and Jean for all their help and support.

The publishers would like to thank Alexandra Clayton for her assistance in the preparation of this book.

Every effort has been made to contact copyright holders of any material reproduced in this book. Any omissions will be rectified in subsequent printings if notice is given to the publishers.

Disclaimer
All the Internet addresses (URLs) given in this book were valid at the time of going to press. However, due to the dynamic nature of the Internet, some addresses may have changed, or sites may have ceased to exist since publication. While the author and publishers regret any inconvenience this may cause readers, no responsibility for any such changes can be accepted by either the author or the publishers.

Contents

Words appearing in bold, **like this**, are explained in the Glossary

Elements and atomic structure

Have you ever wondered how many different substances there are in the world? If you look around, you will see metals, plastics, water and lots of other solids and liquids. You cannot see the gases in the air, but you know they are there, and there are many other gases too. So just how many different substances are there? Incredibly, more than 19 million different substances have been discovered, named and catalogued. Around 4000 substances are added to the list each day, yet all these substances are made from just a few simple substances called **elements**.

Elements

There are 92 naturally occurring elements and a few **artificial** ones, including element number 114 in **group** 4. Elements are substances that cannot be broken down into simpler substances using chemical **reactions**. About three-quarters of the elements are metals, such as copper and gold, and most of the rest are non-metals, such as sulphur and oxygen. Some elements, like germanium, are called metalloids because they have some of the properties of metals and some of the properties of non-metals.

Compounds

Elements can join together in chemical reactions to make **compounds**. For example, copper and oxygen react together to make copper oxide, and sulphur and oxygen react together to make sulphur dioxide. This means that nearly all of the millions of different substances in the world are compounds, made up of two or more elements chemically joined together.

These sailboards are made from some of the millions of known chemicals, including plastics and metals. Seawater and clouds are made from chemicals – and so are the surfers!

Atoms

Every substance is made up of tiny particles called **atoms**. An element is made up of just one type of atom, and a compound is made up of two or more types of atom joined together. Atoms are far too small to see, even with a light microscope. If you could line up copper atoms side by side along a 15 cm ruler, you would need over 535 million of them!

Atoms themselves are made up of even tinier **sub-atomic** particles called **protons**, **neutrons** and **electrons**. At the centre of each atom there is a **nucleus** made up of protons and neutrons. The electrons are arranged in different energy levels around the nucleus. Most of an atom is actually empty space – if an atom were blown up to the same size as an Olympic running track, its nucleus would be about the size of a pea! The electrons, and how they are arranged, are responsible for the ways in which each element can react.

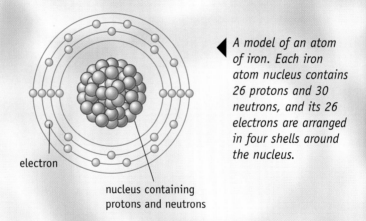

A model of an atom of iron. Each iron atom nucleus contains 26 protons and 30 neutrons, and its 26 electrons are arranged in four shells around the nucleus.

electron

nucleus containing protons and neutrons

Elements and groups

Different elements react with other substances in different ways. Scientists found it difficult to make sense of these chemical reactions. In 1869, a Russian chemist called Dimitri Mendeleev ordered each element into one of eight groups in a table. Each group contained elements with similar chemical properties. This made it much easier for chemists to work out what to expect when they reacted elements with each other. You can find the modern **periodic table** on the next page.

CHAPTER 2

The periodic table and the transition metals

Chemists built on Mendeleev's work and eventually produced the modern **periodic table**, which you can see here. Each row in the table is called a **period**, and the **elements** in a period are arranged in order of increasing **atomic number** (the atomic number is the number of **protons** in the nucleus). Each column in the table is called a **group**. The elements in each group have similar chemical properties to each other. For example, the elements in group 1 are very reactive, soft metals, and the elements in group 0 are very unreactive gases. However, some groups, like group 5, contain both metals and non-metals. It is called the periodic table because these different chemical properties occur regularly, or periodically.

Usually the elements in a group are very similar to each other. This makes it easier to learn about the different elements because you do not have to remember details about each one – you just have to remember the things that apply to a group and the trends in it. However, the transition metals are a bit different.

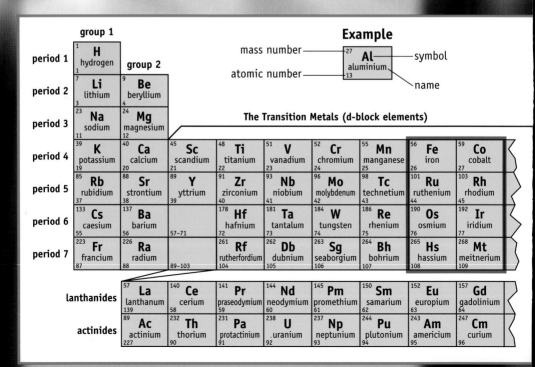

The transition metals

The transition metals are the big block of elements in the middle of the periodic table, between group 2 (the alkaline earth metals) and group 3. They have many properties in common, such as high melting and boiling points, but they are not identical to each other. Tungsten, for example, has the highest melting point of any metal, yet mercury is the only metal that is a liquid at room temperature. The transition metals tend to have high **densities** and they often produce coloured **compounds**. Unlike the other elements in the periodic table, the transition metals in each group may be less like each other, and more like the elements either side of them. However, they do have some things in common, usually the formulae of the compounds they form with other elements.

In this book, you are going to find out about iron, nickel, gold and the other transition metals in the second five groups, the compounds they make and many of their uses.

▼ This is the periodic table of the elements. The transition metals consist of ten groups of elements, which lie between group 2 and group 3.

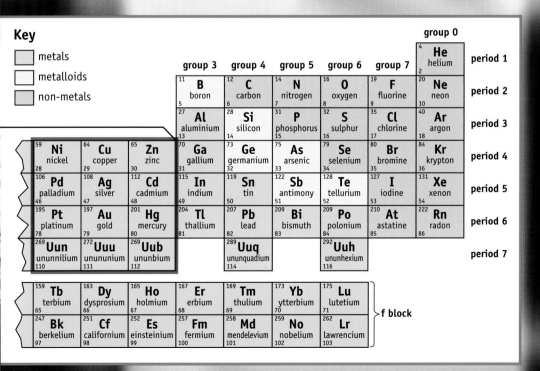

General features of the transition metals

The transition metals are good conductors of electricity and heat. They tend to be hard, strong and tough. Most of them are **malleable**, which means that they are easily bent or hammered into shape. The transition metals are very similar to each other. This is because, apart from zinc, cadmium and mercury in the twelfth group, one of their outer electron shells is not completely filled with electrons. This is called the d sub-shell, and the transition metals belong to a block of elements in the **periodic table** called the d-block.

Most of the other familiar metals are in groups 1 and 2, so it is helpful to see how the transition metals compare with them. Group 1 includes lithium, sodium and potassium, and group 2 includes magnesium and calcium.

High melting and boiling points
Nearly all the transition metals have higher melting and boiling points than the metals in groups 1 and 2. Only zinc, cadmium and mercury melt or boil at lower temperatures.

The boiling points of nearly all the transition metals are much higher than the boiling points of the metals in group 2. The melting points of the metals in group 1 are even lower. ▶

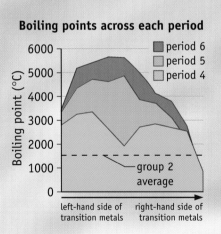

Boiling points across each period

High densities
The **elements** in groups 1 and 2 have low **densities**. Lithium, sodium and potassium will even float on water, but the transition metals generally have high densities. Osmium and iridium have the highest densities of any element, and just three litres of them have the mass of an average adult man!

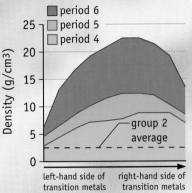

Densities across each period

period 6
period 5
period 4

Density (g/cm³)

25
20
15
10
5
0

group 2
average

left-hand side of
transition metals

right-hand side of
transition metals

The densities of all the transition metals are much higher than the densities of the metals in group 2. The densities of the metals in group 1 are even lower.

Catalysts and colours

Metals lose **electrons** from their outer shells when they react with non-metals, such as oxygen. When they do this, they form electrically charged particles called **ions**. Metal ions are positively charged. Group 1 metals always form ions with a single positive charge, like the Na^+ ions formed by sodium. Group 2 metals always form ions with two positive charges, such as magnesium ions, Mg^{2+}. However, transition metals can form more than one type of ion. As a result, transition metals and their **compounds** frequently make good **catalysts**, which means that they can speed up **reactions** without being used up.

Transition metals can also form different compounds with the same non-metal. For example, iron and oxygen react together to make iron oxide. However, as there are several forms of it, chemists use roman numbers to tell them apart. So, FeO is iron(II) oxide (pronounced 'iron two oxide') and it contains Fe^{2+} ions. However, Fe_2O_3 is iron(III) oxide (pronounced 'iron three oxide') and it contain Fe^{3+} ions. Transition metal compounds are usually coloured because of the way light is absorbed by the ions in them. Iron(II) oxide is black, but iron(III) oxide is red-brown.

The platinum group metals

There are six transition metals that are particularly similar to each other. These are ruthenium, osmium, rhodium, iridium, palladium and platinum. They form a block in the middle of the transition metals and are called the platinum **group** metals after the most abundant member of the group. As you will discover, they are very similar in many ways.

Where are they found? These metals are extremely rare in the Earth's crust. On average there is only a gram of ruthenium in each tonne of rock and barely a gram of rhodium in over a 1000 tonnes of rock! There are few **minerals** that contain platinum group metals in worthwhile amounts, and they are mostly found in South Africa and Russia. The wastes produced from nickel **refining** are also a source of these metals.

What are their main uses? Not only are they very similar to each other, the metals are often mixed together to form natural **alloys**, such as osmiridium (osmium and iridium) and platiniridium (platinum and iridium). This makes it difficult to separate them from one another. However, they are very useful in the manufacture of a variety of highly specialized items.

Catalytic converters

When a hydrocarbon like petrol burns completely in oxygen, the only **products** are carbon dioxide and water vapour. However, in a car engine the amount of air is limited and some of the fuel does not burn completely. As a result, it also produces carbon monoxide and unburnt hydrocarbons, called **volatile** organic compounds or VOCs. In addition, nitrogen and oxygen in the air react together in the hot engine to produce nitrogen oxides, called NOx. These gases pollute the atmosphere when they escape through the exhaust pipe. Carbon monoxide is a poisonous gas, VOCs can react with other gases in the air to cause smog, and NOx can dissolve in clouds to cause acid rain. Car exhaust systems are fitted with catalytic converters to convert these harmful gases into less harmful ones.

The catalytic converter is fixed between the car's engine and silencer in the exhaust system. Its honeycomb structure gives a huge surface area of catalyst in contact with the exhaust gases.

A catalytic converter is a stainless steel can fitted between the engine and the silencer. The **catalyst** inside is made from platinum, rhodium and palladium alloys. Catalytic converters use 41 per cent of the world's production of platinum, 98 per cent of its rhodium and 70 per cent of its palladium. These are expensive metals because they are so rare. To reduce the cost and to provide a big surface area for the gases to react on, the catalysts are coated on to a ceramic honeycomb. The polluting gases are converted into less harmful nitrogen, carbon dioxide and water vapour as they pass through the converter. A modern 'three-way' catalytic converter reduces the three types of polluting gases by up to 90 per cent.

The word equations for some of the reactions in the catalytic converter are:

nitrogen + carbon $\rightarrow$ nitrogen + carbon
oxides   monoxide   dioxide

carbon monoxide + oxygen $\rightarrow$ carbon dioxide

unburnt hydrocarbons + oxygen $\rightarrow$ carbon + water
(VOCs)   dioxide

Eighth group: ruthenium and osmium

101 Ru 44 ruthenium	**ruthenium**
	symbol: Ru • atomic number: 44 • period 5

Ruthenium is a hard, white metal that will only react with oxygen when it is heated strongly. Ruthenium does not react with water or acids, or even with a powerful mixture of concentrated hydrochloric acid and nitric acid called **aqua regia**.

Who discovered it?   Ruthenium was first discovered in 1828 by Gottfried Osann, a chemist working at the University of Tartu in Estonia. He named it after the Latin name for Russia. Unfortunately, Osann took back his claim after Jöns Berzelius, the Swedish chemist who had isolated titanium three years earlier, could not confirm his discovery. In 1844, a Russian chemist called Karl Klaus managed to isolate several grams of ruthenium, so he is usually given the credit for discovering it.

What are its main uses?   Less than a tonne of ruthenium is produced each year. It is used in electronic components called resistors, found in many electrical devices, including computers and mobile phones. Hard disk drives in computers store information on disks that are coated with a magnetic material. The amount of information that can be stored can be increased enormously by adding a layer of ruthenium just three atoms thick!

Ruthenium and its compounds are important **catalysts** used by the oil industry to remove smelly hydrogen sulphide from oil.

190 Os 76 osmium	**osmium**
	symbol: Os • atomic number: 76 • period 6

Osmium is a hard, **brittle** metal with a tinge of blue. It is probably the densest element, although iridium has a very similar **density**. Osmium does not react with water or acids, even with aqua regia. It reacts with oxygen in the air at room temperature to produce osmium(VIII) oxide. This is a solid, but it easily turns into a smelly vapour.

Who discovered it? In 1803, an English chemist called Smithson Tennant discovered and isolated osmium from a sample of impure platinum. He named the new **element** after the Greek word for smell, because of the awful smell made when osmium reacts with the air.

What are its main uses? Only about 150 kilograms of osmium are produced each year. Its main use is in **alloys** with other platinum **group** metals and gold because it makes them much harder. These alloys are used to make tough pen nibs and parts for scientific instruments.

Biologists use osmium(VIII) oxide to prepare specimens for examination using a microscope. To get enough light through a specimen, it must be cut into a very thin slice and stained for anything to show up. Before the specimen can be stained, it must be fixed to stop the cells changing shape. Osmium(VIII) oxide reacts with the fats in cell membranes and fixes them. When it does this, it turns into black osmium(IV) oxide and stains the specimen as well, so it can be examined using a light microscope. Osmium also shows up in electron microscope pictures because it is very dense.

▼ _A blood platelet seen through a transmission electron microscope. You cannot see the membrane itself, just the outline of it where the osmium(VIII) oxide has reacted and stuck to it._

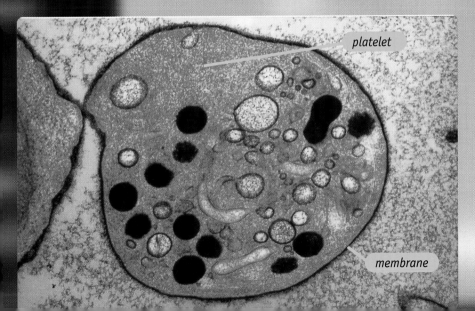

platelet

membrane

Ninth group: rhodium and iridium

103 Rh rhodium 45	**rhodium**
	symbol: Rh • atomic number: 45 • period 5

Rhodium is a hard, silvery metal. It does not react with water and it only reacts with oxygen when heated strongly. Rhodium does not react with acids, including **aqua regia**.

Who discovered it? An English chemist called William Wollaston discovered and isolated rhodium in 1803 from a sample of impure platinum. One of the rhodium compounds Wollaston made was red, so he named the new metal after the Greek word for rose-coloured.

What are its main uses? Although only about 20 tonnes of rhodium are produced each year, it is an important metal. Nearly all of it is used in catalytic converters, but a rhodium–platinum **alloy** is used as the **catalyst** for the industrial production of nitric acid from ammonia. Small amounts of rhodium are often added to platinum and palladium to make alloys that are tougher than the metals on their own. As these alloys have a high melting point and are very unreactive, they are widely used to make laboratory equipment such as crucibles.

192 Ir iridium 77	**iridium**
	symbol: Ir • atomic number: 77 • period 6

Iridium is a silvery-white metal that only reacts with air when it is heated, forming black iridium oxide. It does not react with water or acids, or even with aqua regia.

Who discovered it? Smithson Tennant, an English chemist, discovered and isolated iridium in 1804, from a sample of impure platinum. As iridium makes colourful **compounds**, it is named after Iris, the ancient Greek goddess of rainbows.

What are its main uses? Iridium is the most corrosion-resistant metal of all, but it is difficult to work into shape because it is very hard and **brittle**. As a result, it is usually mixed with platinum to make tough alloys that do not corrode. These alloys are used to make surgical instruments, crucibles for chemists to analyse chemicals, electrical contacts and spark plugs for car engines.

Dinosaurs, meteorites and iridium

Scientists believe iridium may have played a part in the destruction of the dinosaurs. The concentration of iridium in meteorites is over a thousand times more than its concentration in the Earth's crust, and meteorites release a lot of iridium when they crash through the atmosphere into the ground. This eventually settles on the ground, and gives scientists a big clue about when a meteorite might have hit the Earth in the past, and where.

The dinosaurs died out at the end of the Cretaceous period, and there is a lot of iridium in the layer between the rocks from the Cretaceous period and the Tertiary period just after that. Some scientists think that this iridium at the boundary shows that a very large meteorite hit the Earth 65 million years ago. The impact would have thrown up lots of dust into the atmosphere, affecting the climate and helping to drive the dinosaurs to extinction.

◀ *This shows how the Chicxulub basin in the Yucatán Peninsula of Mexico might have looked soon after impact. The 300 km-wide crater has since been filled in.*

Tenth group: palladium and platinum

106	**palladium**
Pd	symbol: Pd • atomic number: 46 • period 5
palladium	
46	

Palladium is a soft, steel-grey metal. It is the most reactive of the platinum group metals and it reacts slowly with concentrated acids. However, it does not react with water and it only reacts with oxygen when it is heated. Palladium can **adsorb** huge amounts of hydrogen gas on its surface, which can be released later just by heating the metal.

Who discovered it? William Wollaston, an English chemist, discovered and isolated palladium in 1803 from a sample of impure platinum. He named it in honour of Pallas (the second largest asteroid), which had only just been found the year before.

These platinum coins were minted in Russia between 1825 and 1855. The platinum was mined in the Ural Mountains, which lie between Europe and Asia.

What are its main uses? Around 200 tonnes of palladium are produced each year. It is used in electronic devices, jewellery and dental bridges and caps. However, most of it is used as a **catalyst**. Its biggest single use as a catalyst is in catalytic converters for car exhausts. It works particularly well in 'hydrogenation' **reactions**, where hydrogen is added to other chemicals. Palladium is the catalyst used to produce hydrogen peroxide, which is widely used in the chemical and paper-making industries.

195 **Pt** platinum 78	**platinum** *symbol: Pt • atomic number: 78 • period 6*

Platinum is a very unreactive, silvery metal. It reacts with **aqua regia**, but it does not react with other acids, air or water.

Who discovered it? The people living in Central America used platinum to make jewellery long before Christopher Columbus discovered America in the 15th century. A Spanish explorer called Antonio de Ulloa described platinum in his journal in 1735, and so is given the credit for its discovery even though the local people had been using it for centuries. In 1805 William Wollaston developed a method to produce platinum in a form that could be easily worked, but he kept his method a secret until 1828 and became a wealthy man as a result.

What are its main uses? Jewellery and catalytic converters are the two biggest uses of platinum, accounting for about 150 tonnes of the metal each year. A platinum **bullion** coin or bar costs about twice as much as the same mass of gold. Like gold, platinum does not tarnish but, unlike gold, it is strong and even very fine pieces keep their shape well. This makes platinum ideal for jewellery, if you can afford it! Platinum in jewellery is usually 95 per cent platinum **alloyed** with copper and other platinum group metals. It can be polished to a highly reflective and attractive finish. About 1 per cent of platinum is hoarded away as bullion coins and bars, but about 40 per cent is made into jewellery.

Although less important in terms of the amount of metal used, platinum is also used in electronic devices and to make different types of laboratory equipment. Cisplatin, a **compound** of platinum, is an important anti-cancer drug.

The artificial transition metals

Uranium **atoms** are the heaviest natural atoms, with 92 **protons** in their nuclei. Atoms with more protons, called transuranic **elements**, have to be made artificially by converting one element into another. The ancient alchemists had tried to turn lead into gold without any success. This was because it is not possible to convert one element into another by chemical **reactions** – you can only turn one element into another by a nuclear reaction.

When a **radioactive** atom **decays**, its **nucleus** splits apart to make a new nucleus and **radiation**. The new element made has a smaller number of particles in its nucleus than the original element. To get a new **artificial** element with a bigger nucleus, you need to smash **ions** into a metal target at high speed and hope that some of them will stick together. Nine artificial transition metals have been made this way but the amounts are so tiny, often just a few atoms, that very little is known about their chemistry. However, chemists predict that they will have similar properties to the other transition metals.

129 **Hs** hassium 108	**hassium** *symbol: Hs • atomic number: 108 • period 7*

Hassium was made in 1984 when scientists fired iron ions at a lead target. Over ten days they managed to produce just three atoms of hassium! Their research was carried out in Darmstadt in the German state of Hesse, and hassium comes from the Latin name for Hesse. Until 1997, hassium was called unniloctium (pronounced 'yoon-nil-oct-ium'), meaning 'one-zero-eight'.

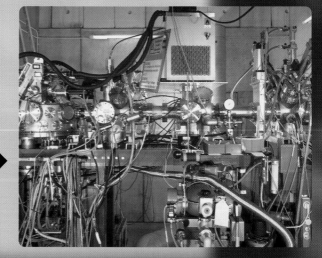

Equipment at the Institute for Heavy Ion Research (GSI) in Darmstadt, Germany. It was here that many of the artificial transition metals were made.

268 **Mt** meitnerium 109	**meitnerium**
	symbol: Mt • atomic number: 109 • period 7

The German team who made hassium were also the first to make meitnerium. They smashed iron ions into a bismuth target over ten days, and succeeded in making a single atom of meitnerium in 1982. The new element was named after one of the discoverers of atomic fission, an Austrian-Swedish physicist called Lise Meitner. Until 1997 it was temporarily called unnilennium (pronounced 'yoon-nil-en-ium'), which means 'one-zero-nine'.

271 **Uun** ununnilium 110	**ununnilium**
	symbol: Uun • atomic number: 110 • period 7

Ununnilium (pronounced 'yoon-oon-nil-ium') was first made in 1994 by firing nickel ions into lead. A tiny number of ununnilium atoms were produced – in one experiment, just one atom was made in a week! Ununnilium is a temporary name that means 'one-one-zero', but the name darmstadtium (chemical symbol Ds) was recommended in 2003, in honour of Darmstadt where the element was first made.

272 **Uun** unununium 111	**unununium**
	symbol: Uuu • atomic number: 111 • period 7

Unununium was first made in 1994 at the Institute for Heavy Ion Research, Darmstadt by bombarding lead with bismuth ions. The temporary name unununium (pronounced 'yoon-oon-oonium') means 'one-one-one'.

285 **Uub** ununbium 112	**ununbium**
	symbol: Uub • atomic number: 112 • period 7

Scientists at the Institute for Heavy Ion Research in Germany produced ununbium in 1996 by bombarding lead with zinc ions. Ununbium (pronounced 'yoon-oon-by-um') is a temporary name that means 'one-one-two'. As only very few atoms of ununbium have been produced, very little is known about its chemistry and, of course so far, it has no practical uses.

The ferromagnetic metals

There are three transition metals that can be magnetized. These are iron, cobalt and nickel, and they are called ferromagnetic metals. Alnico is an **alloy** of these three metals and aluminium, and it makes very strong magnets. Iron, cobalt and nickel have many other uses, too, as you will see.

56		iron
	Fe	symbol: Fe • atomic number: 26 • period 4
26	iron	

Iron is a shiny, light grey metal. Pure iron is quite soft, but it becomes harder and stronger when it is alloyed with other **elements**, such as carbon. Steel often contains less than 1 per cent carbon, but cast iron, which is hard and **brittle**, contains up to 4 per cent carbon. Iron reacts with dilute acids at room temperature, it reacts with oxygen in the air when it is heated, and fine iron wool burns in air. Iron does not react with water if there is no oxygen in it, but it rusts if it is exposed to water and oxygen.

Our most important metal

Iron has been known for thousands of years and it is our most important metal. It is the fourth most abundant element in the Earth's crust, and makes up about 5 per cent of it. It is not found in its **native** state, except in some meteorites, but it can be produced just heating iron **ore** with charcoal in a fire. Its name comes from the Anglo-Saxon word 'iren', and the symbol Fe comes from 'ferrum', which is the Latin word for iron. Australia is the world's biggest producer of iron ores, such as haematite and magnetite, which both contain forms of iron oxide. Iron is produced from these ores by heating them with carbon in a blast furnace.

Magnetite is one of the ▶
most important ores of iron.
The other is haematite.

▲ *The rusting of this iron hull is speeded up by the presence of salt in seawater. A coat of paint keeps air and water away from the iron and prevents further rusting.*

Rusting

Rust is red-brown hydrated iron oxide. It easily flakes off to leave more iron exposed and, under the right conditions, iron objects may completely rust away. Rust spoils the appearance of cars, buildings and equipment. It weakens joints and panels, and the damage caused costs a lot of money to put right. Rusting is usually worse at the seaside because salt speeds up the process.

Iron will not rust if air or water cannot reach it. This is easily achieved by painting the metal, but it does not help if rusting has already started because the rust flakes off, taking the paint with it. Iron and steel can be coated in plastic or other metals, such as chromium, to stop rusting. 'Tin' cans are made from steel coated with tin, and galvanized steel is coated with zinc. As zinc is more reactive than iron, it continues to protect the iron even if it is scratched.
If metal parts are going to move past each other, they are usually oiled or greased because paint would simply rub off.

The blast furnace, iron and steel

Iron is **extracted** from iron **ore** in a huge steel column called a blast furnace, lined with heat-resistant bricks to stop it melting in the heat. The raw materials needed are iron ore, coke, limestone and lots of hot air.

Hot air

The blast furnace needs to be really hot to get the **reactions** going inside it. The fuel used to do this is coke, which is nearly pure carbon and made from coal. It reacts with the oxygen in hot air that is blown into the bottom of the blast furnace, eventually increasing the temperature to about 1600 °C.

Carbon is more reactive than iron, so it can react with iron oxide and remove the oxygen from it if the temperature is high enough. However, carbon monoxide gas actually does this job in the blast furnace. When the coke burns, it produces carbon dioxide. This reacts with more coke to make carbon monoxide gas.

Getting iron from the ore

The hot carbon monoxide gas reacts with the iron oxide in the iron ore. This reaction produces carbon dioxide, iron and a little more heat. The blast furnace is so hot that the iron melts and trickles down to the bottom.

The molten iron contains sandy impurities that must be removed before it is tapped off. Limestone contains calcium carbonate, and this breaks down in the heat of the blast furnace to form calcium oxide and carbon dioxide. The calcium oxide then reacts with the sand, which is mostly silica, to make a slag of calcium silicate. The slag floats on top of the molten iron and is tapped off separately.

The 'Crystal Palace' built for the Great Exhibition of 1851 in London, was built from 3500 tonnes of cast iron, 550 tonnes of wrought iron and contained 300,000 panes of glass. It enclosed nearly a million cubic metres, and amazingly took just nine months to build! ▶

Casting the iron

The molten iron contains up to 4 per cent carbon and other impurities, and some of it is allowed to cool in moulds to produce cast iron. The Victorians in the 19th century used cast iron for all sorts of things, including ships, bridges and buildings. It is hard but **brittle**, so nowadays it is used for less demanding jobs such as manhole covers and railings. Wrought iron is a tough and **malleable** form of iron that is used for forging objects. Most iron is processed further to make steel.

Steel making

To convert iron into steel, various non-metal impurities including carbon must be removed or **reduced**. Molten iron from the blast furnace is mixed with scrap iron and pure oxygen is blown into the mixture. Carbon is oxidized to carbon monoxide gas, which bubbles out of the molten iron. Silicon is oxidized to silica and phosphorus is oxidized to phosphate. These impurities, together with sulphur, are removed by adding calcium oxide, which reacts with them and forms a slag. Other elements, including chromium, nickel and manganese are added to the steel to produce **alloys** such as stainless steel.

Uses of iron

Iron is an important **mineral** in our diet. A person weighing 50 kg contains about 3 g of iron, and nearly all of this is found in the red blood cells. These cells contain haemoglobin, the protein that carries oxygen in the blood. There is an iron **atom** at the heart of each haemoglobin **molecule**. If we do not get enough iron in our diet, we suffer from anaemia. People with anaemia have pale skin and become breathless and dizzy because they are not getting enough oxygen to their cells. Iron(II) sulphate is used in tablets to help people who have anaemia.

Iron and steel

Steel, and concrete reinforced with steel, is widely used in the construction of buildings and bridges. Most modern buildings are built around a framework of steel girders that take the weight of the building. Without steel, buildings made just from brick or stone would need increasingly thicker walls at the bottom, which would limit their height.

Steel is used to make railway lines, vehicles and ships, and all sorts of machines and tools. Around 800 million tonnes of steel are used each year, equivalent to about 125 kg for each person in the world!

▶ *Steel is strong enough for us to build very large buildings, ships and bridges, like this one over the River Tagus, near Lisbon in Portugal.*

Magnets and motors

Electromagnets are made by passing electricity through a coil of wire. If the wire is wrapped around an iron core, the electromagnet becomes much stronger. Magnets made from iron and iron **compounds**, such as barium ferrite, are used in electric motors, dynamos and television tubes. Videotapes and computer disks rely on magnetic fields to store their data, and they are coated with tiny particles of iron oxide.

The Earth's core contains iron and nickel, and movements in it produce the Earth's magnetic field. This is important to life on Earth because it stops dangerous **radiation** from the Sun reaching the ground. Compasses made from magnetized iron rely on the Earth's magnetic field to point to the north. However compasses in steel ships may cause a problem. This is because they are likely to point to the ship's hull instead.

This is a binnacle which houses a ship's compass. It contains pieces of metal that can be adjusted to make sure that the compass points to north correctly.

Catalysts and colour

Ammonia is used to make fertilizers and explosives. It is made by reacting nitrogen and hydrogen in a process called the Haber Process, and iron is the **catalyst** that speeds up the **reaction**. Firework sparklers flash when burnt in air because they contain iron filings.

Iron(III) oxide is red, and when it is very finely powdered it is used in cosmetics. It is also used in 'jewellers' rouge', which is used to gently polish jewellery and precious stones. Prussian Blue is a deep blue solid used in paints. It is formed when iron(III) chloride reacts with another iron compound called potassium hexacyanoferrate(II).

Cobalt

$^{59}_{27}$ Co cobalt	**cobalt**
	symbol: Co • atomic number: 27 • period 4

Cobalt is a silvery-grey metal that is hard but **malleable**. It does not react with oxygen in the air unless it is heated. Cobalt does not react with water, but it will react with steam to produce cobalt oxide when it is heated, and it reacts slowly with acids. Cobalt is one of the three metals that can be made into magnets. The other two 'ferromagnetic' metals, iron and nickel, are found on the left and right of cobalt in the **periodic table**.

Who discovered it?   Minerals containing cobalt have been used for thousands of years to make blue pottery and glass. However, cobalt itself was not discovered until 1735 when Georg Brandt, a Swedish chemist, studied the **ores** used to make blue glass. These were thought to contain bismuth, but by 1739 Brandt was able to isolate a new metal. He called this new metal cobalt, after the name of a mythical German goblin. Cobalt ores often contain arsenic, which makes them poisonous. The arsenic made the miners ill, and German miners believed that an evil goblin called the Kobold put these ores in the mines.

Where is it found?   Cobalt is not found naturally as the free metal, and it makes up just 0.002 per cent of the Earth's crust. Several **minerals** contain cobalt, including linnaeite (cobalt sulphide) and cobaltite (cobalt arsenic sulphide). About 36 thousand tonnes of cobalt ores are mined each year, mostly in Africa and Canada, and cobalt is also **extracted** from wastes produced as a by-product of the nickel and copper industry.

These pieces of silvery-grey cobalt metal ▲
have been extracted from the ores
linnaeite and cobaltite.

Around 20 thousand tonnes of cobalt are produced each year. Several methods are used to extract cobalt. In one method, the cobalt ore is heated strongly in air over several hours to produce cobalt sulphate. This is dissolved and cobalt metal is then produced from it using **electrolysis**.

What are its main uses?   One of the major uses of cobalt is in the manufacture of permanent magnets (the familiar magnets that are not electromagnets). Cobalt is mixed with other metals to produce **alloys** such as alnico, which contains iron, aluminium, nickel and cobalt. Alnico is used to make very strong magnets that keep their magnetism at high temperatures. Alnico magnets are the most widely used permanent magnets and are found in devices such as loudspeakers, microphones and electric guitar pickups. Cobalt is used in 'superalloys' that remain strong even at the high temperatures found in jet engines. It is also used as a **catalyst** for several industrial processes, including removing sulphur from crude oil and in the manufacture of plastics and fibres.

The blue colour in the glaze on this Chinese porcelain from the Ming dynasty (1368–1644) comes from cobalt oxide. Delft pottery from the Netherlands also uses cobalt oxide glaze.

Uses of cobalt

Radioactive cobalt

Isotopes are **atoms** of an **element** with the same number of **protons** and **electrons**, but different numbers of **neutrons**. Natural cobalt is made entirely of one isotope, cobalt-59, but scientists have been able to produce other isotopes **artificially**. One of them, cobalt-60, is very **radioactive**. This means that its **nucleus** can break apart and give off **radiation**. Cobalt-60 produces gamma radiation, which is a powerful form of invisible light.

Each **molecule** of vitamin B_{12} contains a cobalt atom. Vitamin B_{12} is found in milk, meat and fish, and it is needed by our bodies to make red blood cells. Some people have difficulty absorbing vitamin B_{12} and they may suffer from anaemia as a result. To help with their diagnosis, doctors may ask these patients to swallow a small amount of vitamin B_{12} containing radioactive cobalt. This acts as a **tracer**, and lets the doctor find out where the vitamin goes in the patient. There are other uses for radioactive cobalt, too.

The gamma radiation from cobalt-60 is used to sterilize medical equipment for use in operations, and to treat cancer by aiming it at cancerous cells. Engineers use it to inspect metal parts such as jet engine blades. It works a bit like a very powerful X-ray photograph, except it shows up cracks in **welds** rather than broken bones.

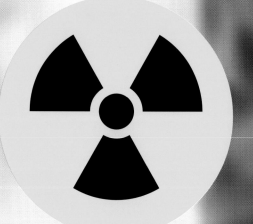

In some countries, food is ▶ *irradiated with gamma rays from cobalt-60 to preserve it. Irradiated food does not become radioactive, but it is often labelled with this international symbol, called the radura. Irradiated food is totally banned in Australia.*

Cobalt compounds

Camcorders and laptop computers need lightweight batteries to power them. Nickel–cadmium (Ni–Cd) batteries are often used, but a lithium-ion battery of the same size can store up to three times as much energy. Lithium cobalt oxide is used to make the **cathode** in lithium-**ion** batteries, which avoids the use of cadmium, a poisonous metal. However, the high cost of cobalt makes lithium-ion batteries much more expensive than Ni–Cd batteries.

Various cobalt **compounds**, including black cobalt oxide, Co_3O_4, and pink cobalt carbonate, are used in glazes for pottery and ceramics. When the pottery is fired in the kiln, these compounds **decompose** or break down to form cobalt oxide, CoO, which is a deep blue colour.

Detecting water

Paper containing cobalt chloride is often used to detect water in laboratory chemicals. It turns deep blue when it is dried in an oven, but turns pink when it is dipped into a substance containing water. Biologists also make use of this **reaction** when they are studying respiration in living things. Respiration is the chemical reaction that releases energy from food, and it happens in all living cells. When you breathe out, your breath contains water vapour, some of which is produced by respiration. If you breathe on a piece of blue cobalt chloride paper, it gradually turns pink because of its reaction with the water vapour in your breath.

Cobalt chloride paper is used to test for water. It is blue when it is dry, but pink when it is damp.

Nickel

59	
Ni	
nickel	
28	

nickel
symbol: Ni • atomic number: 28 • period 4

Nickel is a hard but **malleable** silvery metal. Powdered nickel reacts with oxygen in the air, but lumps of the metal will usually only react when heated. Although it does not react with water or alkalis, nickel reacts with acids to produce coloured nickel salts and hydrogen.

Nickel is used as an industrial **catalyst** *and to add corrosion resistance and strength to steel.* ▶

Who discovered it? **Minerals** containing nickel have been used for hundreds of years to make green glass. However, nickel itself was not discovered until 1751 when Axel Cronstedt, a Swedish chemist, studied one of the **ores** used to make green glass. He dissolved the ore in acid to make a green solution, which he warmed to leave green crystals behind. He produced an impure white metal from these crystals by heating them with carbon. Cronstedt called this metal nickel, after the name of the ore. The ore is now called nickeline, but was originally called kupfernickel, which means devil's copper. This was because, although it looked similar to copper ore, the miners were unable to get any copper out of it, and they believed that the devil was the cause!

Where is it found? Nickel is not found naturally as the free metal, but it makes up 0.007 per cent of the Earth's crust and about 4 per cent of the Earth's core. Luckily, nickel is found in many minerals around the world and it is not necessary to drill down nearly 3000 km to the Earth's core! The main ores are pentlandite (nickel sulphide) and nickeline (nickel arsenide). Russia, Canada and Australia are the main producers, but nickel ores are mined in over twenty countries, and about 1.25 million tonnes of nickel are produced each year.

The nickel ores are crushed and concentrated, then processed to remove some impurities and iron. The impure nickel is reacted with sulphuric acid to make a solution of nickel sulphate. When electricity is passed through this solution, pure nickel forms on the negative electrode.

What are its main uses? Nickel sulphate is used as a **mordant**, which means that it helps dyes stick to textiles. Nickel oxide is used to make the **cathodes** in rechargeable nickel–cadmium batteries, and in powerful long-lasting nickel metal hydride batteries.

Nickel **compounds** must be handled carefully because they are poisonous, while nickel and its **alloys** can cause allergic skin rashes in some people.

▼ These familiar items are made from stainless steel, which resists rusting. About 65 per cent of all nickel is used in making stainless steel.

Uses of nickel

Nickel and margarine

Nickel is used as a **catalyst** in the manufacture of margarine from vegetable oils. These oils are runny at room temperature, but when they are reacted with hydrogen using a nickel catalyst, their melting point increases and they become harder at room temperature. This is what it means when the ingredients include 'hydrogenated vegetable oil'.

Nickel plating

Nickel is coated on to other metals to protect them from rusting, usually by a process called **electroplating**. This involves passing electricity through a bath containing solutions of nickel chloride or nickel nitrate. However, nickel is usually mixed with other metals to form **alloys**.

Nickel alloys

The US five-cent coin, called a 'nickel', is made from a silvery alloy containing 25 per cent nickel and 75 per cent copper. Similar alloys are used in European euro coins. The €2 coin has an inner circle made from nickel covered by an alloy containing 75 per cent copper, 20 per cent zinc and 5 per cent nickel. This is surrounded by a ring made from the alloy used in US nickel pieces. However, the biggest use for nickel is in making stainless steels.

The US 'nickel' and these euro coins contain an alloy of nickel and copper that looks shiny white.

Stainless steels mainly contain iron, chromium and nickel. Those containing between 8 per cent and 14 per cent nickel are easy to clean and so are widely used to make kitchen sinks, worktops and food processing equipment. Stronger stainless steels that resist **corrosion** very well contain less than about 7 per cent nickel. These are used where salt water is involved, such as in equipment to produce fresh water from seawater. Nickel is also found in many other alloys, including heat-resistant 'superalloys' used in jet engines.

Most materials expand when they are heated, and some expand more than others. Invar is an iron–nickel alloy containing 36 per cent nickel. It expands ten times less than iron when it is heated. By altering its composition, its expansion can be made to match other materials. This makes it useful for keeping a gas-tight seal between the glass and metal in electric light bulbs, as both materials expand by the same amount when the bulb warms up.

A flexible alloy

Nitinol is an alloy consisting of 55 per cent nickel and 45 per cent titanium. William Buehler, an American metallurgist, discovered it in 1958. He named it after the symbols of the two metals in it, and the initial letters of the Naval Ordnance Laboratory where he worked. If an object made from Nitinol is bent, it goes back to its original shape when it is warmed. This makes it very useful for making spectacle frames and some surgical instruments and, as it is also very springy, antennas for cell phones.

▼ *Spectacle frames made from Nitinol spring back into shape after being bent.*

Eleventh group: the coinage metals

Because they are relatively unreactive, the metals in the eleventh group, copper, silver and gold, have traditionally been used to make coins.

64	
Cu	
copper	
29	

copper
symbol: Cu • atomic number: 29 • period 4

Copper is a **malleable** metal with a distinctive orange-brown colour. It does not react with oxygen in the air unless it is heated strongly, and it does not react with water or steam. The acids you use at school will not react with copper, but concentrated nitric acid attacks it, forming brown fumes of nitrogen oxide during the **reaction**.

Copper on its own is too soft to be very useful for tools and weapons, so it is usually mixed with other metals to form **alloys**. Bronze is an alloy of copper and tin that is much harder than copper alone, and the Bronze Age began about 6000 years ago when people learnt how to make it. The Romans got most of their copper from the island of Cyprus, and the metal's name comes from the Latin word for Cyprus.

Who discovered it and where is it found? Copper has been known for thousands of years. It can be found in its **native** state as the free metal, but copper is also easy to **extract** from its ores. This is because it is fairly unreactive, so very little energy is needed to produce copper from its **compounds**. Thirteen million tonnes of copper are produced in the world each year from ores such as chalcopyrite, (copper iron sulphide) and cuprite (copper oxide).

Although copper can be found in its native state, it is only rarely found like this now. All the best ores have already been mined, and most copper ores contain less than 2 per cent copper.

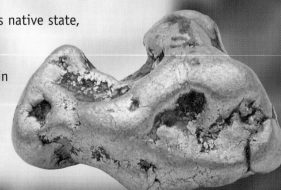

This is a natural nugget or lump of copper metal. ▶

This means that there is a lot of waste rock to be removed before the copper can be extracted, and a process called flotation separation is used to do this. The copper ore is crushed to a fine powder, mixed with water and lots of air is bubbled through it. The unwanted rock sinks to the bottom, while a froth containing copper compounds forms at the surface. The froth is concentrated and dried, and it is often mixed with scrap copper before being processed by roasting it in air. The copper is then purified using **electrolysis**.

It is possible that Neolithic people isolated copper by accident when they surrounded their cooking fires with colourful lumps of copper ore, such as green malachite (copper carbonate). In the heat of the fire, the copper carbonate would easily decompose or break down to form black copper oxide:

$$\text{copper carbonate} \xrightarrow{\text{heat}} \text{copper oxide + carbonate dioxide}$$

Carbon in the fuel would then reduce the copper oxide to shiny copper metal:

$$\text{copper oxide + carbon} \rightarrow \text{copper + carbon dioxide}$$

Carbon is more reactive than copper, so it can remove the oxygen from copper oxide.

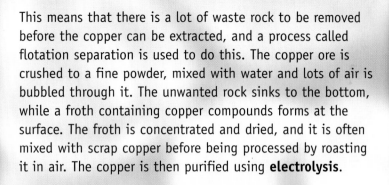

◀ The Statue of Liberty in New York is made from a skin of copper sheeting riveted on to a steel frame. As the copper weathers and reacts with gases in the atmosphere, a protective green 'patina' containing basic copper carbonate and basic copper sulphate forms on its surface.

Uses of copper

Copper against disease

Arthritis is a painful disease in which your joints become swollen and difficult to move. Many people with arthritis wear copper bracelets because they believe that the copper eases the symptoms of the disease, but there is no scientific evidence showing this.

Legionnaire's disease is a serious lung disease that kills up to a fifth of the people who get it. It is caused by a bacterium called *Legionella pneumophila*, which is spread by contaminated water droplets from air conditioning systems. These systems may contain devices that release copper ions and silver ions into the water, which kills the harmful bacteria.

Copper metal and its alloys

Copper is the second best conductor of electricity after silver, and about one hundred times cheaper, so it is widely used in the electrical and electronics industries. It is used in some radiators to carry away waste heat because it is also a good heat conductor and, as it does not react with water, it is used in the plumbing industry for pipes and fittings.

As it is quite unreactive, copper is used on its own or mixed with other metals to make **alloys** that stay shiny. Nickel silver, an alloy of copper, zinc and nickel, is used to make costume jewellery and 'silver' coins. Screws, propellers and musical instruments such as trumpets are often made from brass (copper and zinc), while statues, bells and coins are often made from bronze (copper and tin). Special tools that can be used without causing accidental sparks are made from beryllium–copper alloys. These non-sparking tools are needed in dusty factories, where a stray spark could cause an explosion.

Copper compounds

Copper(II) oxide, CuO, is used to make blue or green glazes for pottery. Copper nitrate is added to the gunpowder in fireworks to make the flame burn with a blue-green colour.

Copper sulphate is needed during the **refining** of copper itself, but its main use is in agriculture. It is an ingredient of wood preservatives and fungicides such as 'Bordeaux mixture', the traditional treatment for grapes used for wine-making.

Food tests

Some sugars, such as glucose and fructose, can react with copper sulphate solution under the right conditions. These sugars are called reducing sugars and they can be detected using a mixture called Benedict's reagent. This contains sodium citrate and sodium carbonate in addition to copper sulphate. It is a clear blue solution, but if it is mixed with these sugars and warmed up, it forms a **precipitate** of solid red copper(I) oxide, Cu_2O. A similar change happens when Fehling's solution, which also contains copper sulphate, is heated with these sugars.

Proteins can be detected using the Biuret test. The test substance is mixed with sodium hydroxide solution, and then some copper sulphate solution is added. If there is any protein in the test substance, the mixture turns purple.

◀ *Copper is a good, relatively cheap conductor of heat that does not react with water. It is ideal for use in central heating systems.*

Silver

108		silver
Ag		symbol: Ag • atomic number: 47 • period 5
silver		
47		

Silver is a shiny white metal. It is quite unreactive, and does not react with air or water unless they are contaminated with corrosive chemicals such as hydrogen sulphide. Silver does not react with dilute acids, but it will react with concentrated sulphuric and nitric acids, especially when it is heated.

Who discovered it?   Silver has been known for thousands of years, and it has been widely used for coins, jewellery and expensive ornaments. The Romans used silver coins, and the symbol for silver comes from the Latin word 'argentum', which means silver. Its name comes from the Anglo-Saxon word for silver.

Where is it found?   Silver makes up a tiny proportion of the Earth's crust, and on average there is less than a gram of it in every 20 tonnes of rock. However, it is found as the free metal and in many **minerals**. The most important silver **ore** is acanthite, also called argentite, which contains silver sulphide. Minerals that contain copper, lead or zinc sulphides usually contain small amounts of silver. Galena, lead sulphide, is one of the most important sources of silver as it can contain up to 1 per cent silver. About three-quarters of the silver produced comes from the wastes left behind after **refining** copper, lead or zinc.

Mexico, Peru, the USA, Australia and Canada are the major sources of silver, and about 18,000 tonnes of silver are produced in the world each year. Depending on the starting material, different methods are used to **extract** it, and all involve several complex steps to produce pure silver.

*Native silver (twisted, wire-like formations) on a rock. It is usually found as a **compound** in minerals such as argentite and horn silver, although it may be found alone, as here.* ▶

▲ American Eagle silver dollar coins, like this one, are 4 cm in diameter and are made from 99.9 per cent silver.

Money, money, money

Silver has been used to make coins since Roman times. However, the value of the silver in coins has become greater than the face value of the coins themselves. Modern 'silver' coins often use a copper-nickel **alloy** that has a silvery appearance. If these coins were made from the same mass of silver, the metal itself would be worth over 20 times the face value of the coin!

Silver coins are still made, but mostly for investors who want to put their savings into buying valuable metals. Silver **bullion** bars are also sold. On its own silver scratches easily, so copper is usually added to it to make it harder. American Eagle coins are made from a silver–copper alloy containing just 0.07 per cent copper, and British Britannia coins are made from Britannia silver, which is 95.8 per cent silver. However, both coins contain 31.1 g (1 ounce) of silver.

Silver–copper alloys are also used in jewellery. You can choose from different jewellery alloys, depending on how much money you have to spend. Sterling silver contains 92.5 per cent silver, and costs more than jewellery silver, which contains only 80 per cent silver.

Uses of silver

Silver is the best conductor of electricity. It is widely used on its own, or alloyed with palladium or zinc, in printed circuit boards and electrical contacts. Metal parts are often joined together using silver solders, which are **alloys** of silver, copper and zinc. Silver is a relatively poor **catalyst** compared to the other transition metals. However, it is ideal for controlling the potentially explosive **reaction** that the chemical industry uses to produce epoxyethane. This is an important **compound** that is used to make car antifreeze, polyesters and detergents. Some silver compounds are very important, too.

Chemical testing

Silver nitrate dissolves in water, unlike most other silver compounds. Chemists use silver nitrate solution to test their chemicals to see if there are any chlorides, such as sodium chloride, dissolved in them. Silver nitrate reacts with chlorides to produce white silver chloride. This does not dissolve in water, so it forms a cloudy white **precipitate**.

The word equation for using silver nitrate solution to find out if a liquid contains dissolved sodium chloride (common salt) is:

silver + sodium → sodium + silver
nitrate   chloride   nitrate   chloride

Sodium nitrate dissolves in water, so you do not see it, but silver chloride forms a cloudy white precipitate because it does not dissolve in water. Chemists usually add a little nitric acid before they add the silver nitrate solution.

Silver nitrate solution can also be used to test for bromides and iodides. Bromides produce a cream coloured precipitate with silver nitrate, and iodides produce a yellow precipitate.

Photography

Silver chloride, bromide and iodide gradually turn black if they are left in the light. This is because the light causes them to **decompose** or break down to form tiny particles of silver that look black. An English scientist called William Fox Talbot discovered how to make photographs using this reaction in the early part of the 19th century. Talbot coated some paper with silver chloride, covered it with an object such as a leaf, and then exposed it to light. Where the paper was exposed to the light, the silver chloride turned black, but where it was covered up it stayed white.

Talbot patented his method in 1841, but photography has developed considerably since then. Many advances have been made in the chemistry of photography, but it remains the biggest single use for silver. Silver chloride, silver bromide and silver iodide are all used in photographic printing papers and films. However, as digital photography becomes more important, the demand for silver for photography is likely to go down.

◀ *A photograph made using William Fox Talbot's talbotype (calotype) method, which uses silver salts.*

Batteries

Silver(I) oxide, with a little manganese(IV) oxide and graphite added to conduct electricity, is used to make the **cathode** in silver-zinc batteries. These produce a lot of energy for their mass, so they are widely used in spacecraft, cameras, watches and so on.

◀ *These small 'button' batteries contain silver oxide. They are used to power watches, calculators and cameras.*

Gold

197		
Au		**gold**
gold		symbol: Au • atomic number: 79 • period 6
79		

Gold is a dense metal with a distinctive rich yellow colour. It does not react with air, water or steam, but it will react with chlorine. The acids you use at school will not react with gold, but a mixture of hydrochloric acid and concentrated nitric acid, called **aqua regia**, will dissolve gold.

Who discovered it?   Gold is very rare, making up just a small 0.000 0003 per cent of the Earth's crust. However, it can be found in its natural state as the free metal, and it is often already very pure. As a result, gold has been known and valued highly for thousands of years. Medieval alchemists spent fruitless centuries trying to turn lead into gold, and wars have been started and civilizations have fallen to satisfy the desire for the shiny, unreactive metal.

Gold rush!

Pieces of gold can be washed out of rocks into rivers and streams. These 'nuggets' can be isolated by 'panning'. Some material from the riverbed is scooped into a shallow dish, which is then swirled gently in the water. Gold is very dense, so it stays in the bottom of the pan while the less dense sand and pebbles are washed out. Of course, there needs to be enough gold in the riverbed to make panning worthwhile! In the Californian Gold Rush of 1849, a quarter of a million people eventually headed west to try to make their fortune, but only a few became rich.

Gold has been highly prized for thousands of years. This statue of Buddha was crafted hundreds of years ago. ▶

▲ *Nuggets of gold are often found in streams and riverbeds where the rain has washed them out of the rocks.*

Where is it found? About 1500 tonnes of gold are produced in the world each year, mainly in South Africa. There are some **minerals** that contain gold, such as calaverite (gold telluride), but most gold is found in its **native** form mixed with rock. The gold is **extracted** using two main methods.

Mercury can dissolve many other metals to form **alloys** called amalgams. When minerals containing gold are mixed with mercury, the gold dissolves to form an amalgam. This is filtered to remove the undissolved impurities. The amalgam is then heated to drive off the mercury, leaving purified gold behind.

In the second method, the minerals are added to sodium cyanide solution. This reacts with the gold to make sodium cyanoaurite solution, which is a gold **compound**. The solution is then filtered to remove the undissolved impurities. When zinc powder is added, it reacts with the sodium cyanoaurite to produce solid gold.

What are its main uses? Gold forms a few compounds even though it is very unreactive. Potassium cyanoaurite is used for gold-plating metal objects using electricity, and some photographers use chlorauric acid to adjust the appearance of their photographs. People with inflamed joints caused by arthritis may get some relief from pain if they receive regular injections of a gold compound called sodium aurothiomalate.

Uses of gold

The biggest industrial use of gold is in the manufacture of electronic equipment. It is nearly as good as copper at conducting electricity, but is less reactive and does not tarnish at all, so it is used to make electrical contacts and fine wires to connect computer chips. If you have failed to look after your teeth properly (and you have plenty of money) you might decide to get a gold filling. These are soft enough not to wear away the other teeth, they do not chip or tarnish and they give you a flashy smile!

▲ Visors on space suits worn by astronauts have a thin layer of gold to reflect infrared radiation.

Gold reserves

Gold is a very expensive metal because it is so rare. Pure gold is too soft for most purposes, so it is often alloyed with other metals such as silver and copper. The proportion of gold in an **alloy** is measured in **carats**: pure gold is 24 carat gold, whereas an alloy containing 50 per cent gold is 12 carat gold. The cheapest jewellery gold is usually 9 carat gold, but more expensive jewellery gold, such as 18 carat gold, is also popular. Coinage gold usually contains a small amount of silver, but the amount varies from country to country. British Sovereigns and American Eagles are 22 carat gold (91.67 per cent gold), but Canadian Maple Leafs are made with 'Four Nines' gold, which is 99.99 per cent gold! The price of gold varies, but typically a coin that contains 31.1 g of gold (one troy ounce) costs hundreds of euros or dollars.

For wealthy people and governments, gold can be stored and traded as **bullion** bars. The 'London Good Delivery Bar' is the size usually stored by central banks, and it weighs 12.5 kg! Huge amounts of gold are stored by governments in their 'gold reserves', including over 8000 tonnes in the USA alone.

Thin gold

Gold is extremely **ductile** and **malleable**. Just 1 g of it could be stretched into a wire over 2 km long and it can be hammered into sheets just 0.02 mm thick! This gold leaf, as it is known, is used to decorate books, fine art and furniture. Gold is a very good heat reflector, so satellites and space probes are often coated with it to protect them while in space. Astronauts' visors and the glass in some buildings are also examples of the use of gold as a heat reflector.

Twelfth group: zinc, cadmium, mercury

The last group contains zinc, cadmium and mercury. Although they are usually included in the transition metals, their d sub-shells are completely filled with electrons, so they do not behave as transition metals at all.

65	
Zn	**zinc**
zinc	symbol: Zn • atomic number: 30 • period 4
30	

Zinc is a blue-white metal that is **brittle** at room temperature but becomes more easily worked above 100 °C. It reacts with acids but it does not react with water. Zinc reacts with the oxygen in damp air and gradually turns grey-black, and it burns in air to produce zinc oxide when it is heated.

Who discovered it? Zinc was first recognised as an **element** in 1789 by the French chemist, Antoine Lavoisier. He wrote an important book on chemistry in which he listed the elements known at the time. Lavoisier did not get it all correct, though – he included light and heat in his list! However, people had known about zinc and its **compounds** for thousands of years before then.

▲

These pieces of pure zinc are extracted from the ores sphalerite or zinc blende (zinc sulphide) and smithsonite (zinc carbonate).

Calamine and brass

Calamine (zinc carbonate) was used by the Romans to cure skin diseases. They also made brass, an **alloy** of zinc and copper, by heating charcoal, zinc carbonate and copper together. It is very difficult to **extract** zinc from its **ores**, but by the 14th century, thousands of tonnes of zinc were being produced in India. In 1743, William Champion started the first commercial European production of zinc at Bristol in England.

Calamine lotion contains zinc carbonate. It helps to soothe the itching you get if you are bitten by an insect or have chickenpox.

Where is it found? Zinc is the 23rd most abundant element in the Earth's crust and makes up about 0.007 per cent of it. Although zinc is not found naturally as the free metal, it is found all over the world in several **minerals**. The main zinc ores are zinc blende and sphalerite (zinc sulphide), and smithsonite (zinc carbonate). Ores containing about nine million tonnes of zinc are mined each year, mainly in Australia and China, but the USA and Canada also produce significant amounts.

There are two main ways to extract zinc, and in each case the zinc ores are first roasted in air to produce zinc oxide.

The word equation for the production of zinc oxide from zinc sulphide ore is:

zinc sulphide + oxygen → zinc oxide + sulphur dioxide

The sulphur dioxide produced in the reaction is used to make sulphuric acid.

If the zinc is going to be extracted by **electrolysis**, the zinc oxide is reacted with sulphuric acid to produce a solution of zinc sulphate. When electricity is passed through this, pure zinc metal forms at the negative **electrode**.

The second method involves heating the zinc oxide in a furnace with coke, a cheap form of nearly pure carbon. This produces carbon dioxide and impure zinc metal. Zinc has a low boiling point for a metal, 907 °C, so it can be purified by distillation. The impure zinc is heated until it turns into a gas. This is separated from the impurities, and then cooled and solidified.

Uses of zinc

Musical instruments such as the alto saxaphone shown here are made from brass, an alloy of zinc and copper.

Zinc is widely used to coat other metals, such as steel. This is called galvanizing, and it is so important that about half of all the zinc produced is used in this way. Zinc melts at just 420 °C, so steel is easily galvanized just by dipping it into a bath of molten zinc. As zinc is more reactive than iron, it **corrodes** before the iron in the steel does. This is called **sacrificial protection** because the zinc 'sacrifices' itself to save the steel. The steel is protected even if the layer of zinc is scratched, so galvanized steel has a huge number of uses, including cars, buildings, bridges and roofs.

Zinc alloys

Brass, an **alloy** containing copper and 20 per cent to 45 per cent zinc, is the oldest zinc alloy. It is easily worked into shape but harder than copper on its own, it does not rust and it conducts electricity well. Brass is used to make electrical and plumbing fittings, screws, equipment for boats, and scientific instruments such as telescopes.

Zinc and aluminium form a strong alloy with a low melting point. This allows it to be moulded into complex shapes in a process called diecasting. Diecast objects are found in parts for cars, aircraft and household appliances. When zinc and lead are mixed together, they produce alloys with low melting points. These are use as solders to join pipes and electrical components. As relatively little heat is needed to melt the solder, the electrical components are not damaged when they are joined.

The first practical battery was the Leclanché cell, named after Georges Leclanché, the French engineer who invented it in 1866. It used zinc and carbon **electrodes**, and ordinary modern batteries, including many alkaline batteries, also use zinc alloy electrodes.

Zinc compounds

Zinc oxide is a white powder used in lotions, bandages and cosmetics because it helps to soothe and heal damaged skin. When you were a baby, your bottom was probably protected by a zinc oxide cream each time you had your nappy changed! Now you are older, you are more likely to come across zinc oxide mixed with titanium(IV) oxide in sunblock preparations.

Zinc sulphide is a **phosphor**, which means that it gives off light after being exposed to **radiation** or light. It is used in luminous paints and toys that glow in the dark, fluorescent lights and television screens. When radioactivity was first discovered, scientists used a device called a spinthariscope to detect the radiation coming off **radioactive** substances. It consisted of a tube with the radioactive substance at one end and a screen coated with zinc sulphide at the other end. To measure how radioactive the substance was, the scientist counted the tiny flashes of light on the screen caused by the radiation.

◄ When taking part in outdoor pursuits it is advisable to wear sunblock on the exposed parts of your face to protect them from the Sun's harmful rays.

Cadmium

112 Cd cadmium 48	**cadmium** symbol: Cd • atomic number: 48 • period 5

Cadmium is a silvery-white metal with a bluish tinge. It is soft and easily cut with a knife. The melting and boiling points of cadmium are quite low for a metal, and it produces a yellow vapour when heated. Cadmium is very similar chemically to zinc, which is immediately above it in the **periodic table**. It does not react with water or alkalis, but it reacts with hot acids and it burns in air when heated to form brown cadmium oxide. The metal and its **compounds** are very poisonous, so they need to be handled with great care. Despite this, they have many uses, including the manufacture of batteries and television sets.

Who discovered it? Cadmium was discovered in 1817 by the German chemist, Friedrich Stromeyer. He studied a **mineral** that contained zinc carbonate. Zinc carbonate is white, and when it is heated it **decomposes** or breaks down to form zinc oxide. This is yellow when it is hot, but it turns white when it cools down. However, the mineral that Stromeyer studied turned orange when it was heated, and it stayed that way. He decided that it must contain another metallic **element** besides zinc, and eventually he managed to isolate a previously unknown metal.

Friedrich Stromeyer, who discovered cadmium. He called the new element cadmium, after cadmia, the name of the mineral from which it came.

Where is it found? About 1800 tonnes of cadmium are produced in the world each year, but almost none of it comes from a cadmium **ore**. Cadmium makes up only just 0.000 02 per cent of the Earth's crust. It is not found naturally as the free metal and cadmium ores are very rare. The only commercially valuable cadmium ore is greenockite, which contains cadmium sulphide. Greenockite is named after Lord Greenock who owned the land in Scotland where it was first discovered.

The word equations for the production of cadmium from cadmium sulphide are:

cadmium + oxygen → cadmium + sulphur
sulphide   oxide   dioxide

cadmium oxide + carbon → cadmium + carbon dioxide

Zinc ores contain tiny amounts of cadmium, so most cadmium is extracted from the by-products of zinc refining. Zinc ores, such as sphalerite (zinc sulphide), are roasted in air to produce zinc oxide. This is then heated strongly with coke, which is mostly carbon, to produce zinc. If the original ore contained a little cadmium, this will be mixed with the zinc. The two metals have very different boiling points, so they can be separated from each other by distillation.

◄ *These are nuggets of pure cadmium. The metal is often associated with zinc ores such as sphalerite (zinc sulphide) and also occurs as the mineral greenockite (cadmium sulphide).*

Uses of cadmium

The surfaces of steel and aluminium coated with cadmium have a lower friction than the uncoated metals. This means that metal parts coated with cadmium can slide over each other more easily. As a result, some moving parts in cars and aircraft may be coated with cadmium. Cadmium also protects steel from rusting, just as zinc does.

Small amounts of cadmium metal are often mixed with other metals to make **alloys**. Copper alloyed with about 1 per cent cadmium is twice as strong as copper on its own, and it is widely used for telephone cables and car radiators. Cadmium also lowers the melting point of some alloys. Woods metal is a very unusual alloy because it melts at just −70 °C, which is less than the temperature of a fresh cup of tea! It is made from a mixture of bismuth, lead, tin and 12.5 per cent cadmium. Woods metal is used in the valves of automatic sprinkler systems found in the ceilings of shops and factories. If there is a fire, the metal valve melts and releases water over the flames.

▲ *Aircraft engine parts may be coated with cadmium to reduce the friction between moving parts and to resist rusting.*

Pigments and plastics

Cadmium sulphide and cadmium selenium sulphide are used to make yellow, orange and red **pigments** for artists' paints. As these pigments keep their colours at high temperatures, they are often used in paints for the pipes in chemical factories, and in coloured glass. Small amounts of cadmium pigments are added to plastics, including poly(ethene) and nylon, to make objects such as bright yellow gas pipes.

Polyvinyl chloride, PVC, gradually becomes **brittle** when it is exposed to the **ultraviolet light** in sunshine. To help prevent this damage, small amounts of chemicals called stabilizers are added to the plastic when it is being made. Cadmium stearate is frequently used as a stabilizer.

Electronics and batteries

Cadmium sulphide is used to make light-sensitive electronic devices, including solar cells, photocopier systems and camera exposure meters. It is a **phosphor**, which means that it gives off light when it is exposed to **radiation** such as **electron** beams, and it provides the green colour in television pictures.

Nickel-cadmium batteries containing cadmium and cadmium hydroxide account for over two-thirds of the cadmium used. These batteries are often called 'nicads' from Ni–Cd, the chemical symbols for nickel and cadmium. Rechargeable Ni–Cd batteries are widely used in cellphones, laptop computers and other portable electrical equipment. Large industrial Ni-Cd batteries are used to supply emergency power in case of an electricity failure, and they are also used to power the starter motors for trains and aircraft.

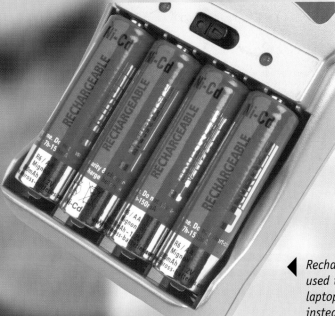

◀ *Rechargeable Ni–Cd batteries are used to power camcorders and laptop computers, and are useful instead of ordinary batteries in toys.*

Mercury

201 Hg mercury 80	**mercury** *symbol: Hg • atomic number: 80 • period 6*

Mercury is a silvery metal with a very interesting property – it is the only metal that is liquid at room temperature. As it is nearly fourteen times denser than water, metal objects will float on the surface of the liquid form. Mercury is highly poisonous to all living things, so great care must be taken when handling it.

Mercury does not react with water or hydrochloric acid, but it reacts with concentrated nitric acid and dissolves in boiling sulphuric acid. If it is heated above about 350 °C, mercury reacts with oxygen in the air to form mercury oxide, which is a red solid. It dissolves most other metals to form special **alloys**, called amalgams. Amalgam tooth fillings are made from mercury, silver and tin.

Who discovered it? Mercury has been known for thousands of years, as it is easily extracted from its main **ore**, cinnabar, simply by heating it in air. The cinnabar mines at Almadén in Spain have been in use for 6000 years.

Quicksilver

Mercury is named after a Roman god called Mercurius, and it was also known as quicksilver, which means 'alive silver'. The chemical symbol Hg comes from 'hydrargyrum', the Greek for 'water silver'. The Romans were well aware of its dangers, and condemned prisoners to work in the cinnabar mines, where the poisonous metal would usually kill them within three years!

▲

If mercury is poured into a glass dish and swirled around, the glass does not get 'wet' but droplets of the metal easily break away from each other, only to join back up again.

Where is it found? Mercury is quite rare in the Earth's crust and only forms about 0.000 05 per cent of it. However, there are more than 20 minerals that contain mercury, including cinnabar (mercury sulphide), and it is sometimes found in its **native** form as the free metal. About 1400 tonnes of mercury are **extracted** in the world each year, and more than a third of this comes from Spain. To extract the mercury, crushed cinnabar is mixed with a stream of hot air. The oxygen in the air reacts with the sulphur in the cinnabar to form sulphur dioxide, and the mercury is released as mercury vapour. The vapour is led away and cooled so that it condenses to form liquid mercury metal.

What are its main uses? Like most liquids, mercury expands when it is warmed. It does this in a regular way, allowing very accurate thermometers for measuring temperature to be made. At school you are likely to use alcohol thermometers, because if a mercury thermometer is accidentally broken special procedures are needed to make sure no one is affected and that the poisonous metal is disposed of.

You are also not allowed to carry anything containing mercury on to an aircraft because aircraft are made from aluminium alloys. If the mercury escapes, it will dissolve the aluminium to make an amalgam and damage the aircraft.

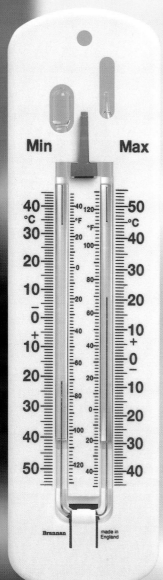

◄ *A German physicist called Gabriel Fahrenheit invented the alcohol thermometer in 1709 and the mercury thermometer five years later.*

Uses of mercury

Barometers

Barometers measure atmospheric pressure. An Italian physicist called Evangelista Torricelli invented the mercury barometer in 1643 when he filled a long glass tube with mercury, then turned it upside down in a dish of mercury. He found that the mercury ran out of the tube until about 760 mm was left in it. The pressure of the air on the mercury in the dish pushed the mercury up the tube and kept it there.

If the air pressure goes down, so does the column of mercury in a barometer. Barometers can give you some warning of changes to the weather because different types of weather are associated with different air pressures. If the air pressure goes up, the weather is likely to be fine, but if it goes down it is likely to bring rain.

Mercury compounds

Mercury(II) oxide, HgO, is a yellow-red solid that is used to make other mercury **compounds**. If it is heated, it easily breaks down to produce mercury and oxygen, a **reaction** that led to the discovery of oxygen by Joseph Priestley in 1774. Mercury oxide mixed with graphite is one of the electrodes in zinc–mercury oxide batteries, which often power hearing aids. However, just like the metal itself, mercury compounds are very poisonous. They can cause birth defects, and damage to the kidneys and brain.

Minamata disease

In 1956, fishermen and their families in the southern Japanese city of Minamata began to fall ill. They found it difficult to move properly, and suffered headaches and slurred speech. Thousands of people became ill and many died. The cause turned out to be mercury poisoning from eating contaminated fish caught in Minamata Bay.
A local chemical company used mercury as a **catalyst** to make ethanal, a raw material for making plastics. Unfortunately, methyl mercury was also made in the process. It was discharged into the bay in waste water and about

200 tonnes of mercury ended up in the sea. Once there, it built up in the food chain in larger and larger amounts in a process called bioaccumulation. Tiny animals and plants absorbed it and were then eaten by small fish. These fish became contaminated themselves, and were eaten by larger fish that absorbed even more methyl mercury. People eating the fish received the largest dose of mercury and became seriously ill as a result. After the cause was discovered, the bay was dredged to remove the contaminated sediment, and many years later it is now safe to eat fish caught there.

▼ *The people of Minamata protested against the dumping of waste mercury compounds into their bay. Many of them had suffered mercury poisoning after eating fish caught there.*

Find out more about the transition metals

Elements

The table below contains some further information about the properties of the transition metals in this book. The artificial **elements** have only been made in tiny amounts, often only a few **atoms**, so very little is known about their properties.

Element	Symbol	Atomic number	Melting point (°C)	Boiling point (°C)	Density (g/cm³)
cadmium	Cd	48	321	766	8.6
cobalt	Co	27	1495	2870	8.9
copper	Cu	29	1083	2567	8.9
gold	Au	79	1064	2807	19.3
iridium	Ir	77	2407	4130	22.5
iron	Fe	26	1536	2750	7.9
mercury	Hg	80	−39	357	13.5
nickel	Ni	28	1453	2732	8.9
osmium	Os	76	3054	5027	22.6
palladium	Pd	46	1554	3140	12.0
platinum	Pt	78	1772	3827	21.5
rhodium	Rh	45	1966	3727	12.4
ruthenium	Ru	44	2310	3900	12.4
silver	Ag	47	962	2212	10.5
zinc	Zn	30	420	907	7.1

The following elements can be found in *The Transition Metals I: Tungsten, Titanium and Other Elements.*

Element	Symbol	Element	Symbol
bohrium	Bh	scandium	Sc
chromium	Cr	seaborgium	Sg
dubnium	Db	tantalum	Ta
hafnium	Hf	technetium	Tc
manganese	Mn	titanium	Ti
molybdenum	Mo	tungsten	W
niobium	Nb	vanadium	V
rhenium	Re	yttrium	Y
rutherfordium	Rf	zirconium	Zr

Compounds

These tables show you the chemical formulas of a selection of the **compounds** mentioned in the book. For example, nickel sulphate has the formula $NiSO_4$. This means it is made from one nickel atom, one sulphur atom and four oxygen atoms, joined together by chemical bonds.

Cadmium compounds	formula
cadmium hydroxide	$Cd(OH)_2$
cadmium oxide	CdO
cadmium sulphide	CdS

Cadmium compounds

Cobalt compounds	formula
cobalt chloride	$CoCl_2$
cobalt oxide	Co_3O_4
cobalt sulphate	$CoSO_4$
cobalt sulphide	CoS
cobalt(II) oxide	CoO

Cobalt compounds

Copper compounds	formula
copper carbonate	$CuCO_3$
copper chloride	$CuCl_2$
copper sulphate	$CuSO_4$
copper(I) oxide (red)	Cu_2O
copper(II) oxide (black)	CuO

Copper compounds

Gold compounds	formula
chlorauric acid	$HAuCl_4$
gold telluride	$AuTe_2$

Gold compounds

Iridium compounds	formula
iridium oxide	IrO_2

Iridium compounds

Find out more continued

Iron compounds

Iron compounds	formula
iron(II) chloride	$FeCl_2$
iron(III) chloride	$FeCl_3$
iron(III) oxide (haematite)	Fe_2O_3
magnetite	Fe_3O_4

Mercury compounds

Mercury compounds	formula
mercury(II) oxide	HgO
mercury sulphide	HgS

Nickel compounds

Nickel compounds	formula
nickel chloride	$NiCl_2$
nickel oxide	NiO
nickel sulphate	$NiSO_4$
nickel sulphide	NiS

Osmium compounds

Osmium compounds	formula
osmium(IV) oxide	OsO_2
osmium(VIII) oxide	OsO_4

Platinum compounds

Platinum compounds	formula
platinum arsenide (sperrylite)	$PtAs_2$
cisplatin	$Cl_2H_6N_2Pt$

Silver compounds

Silver compounds	formula
silver nitrate	$AgNO_3$
silver sulphide	Ag_2S
silver(I) oxide	Ag_2O

Zinc compounds

Zinc compounds	formula
zinc oxide	ZnO
zinc sulphate	$ZnSO_4$
zinc sulphide	ZnS

Glossary

adsorb when a chemical sticks to a surface

alpha radiation (α radiation) radiation caused by quickly moving helium nuclei which have broken away from an unstable nucleus

alloys mixtures of two or more metals, or mixtures of a metal and a non-metal. Alloys are often more useful than the pure metal on its own.

amalgam mixture formed when mercury dissolves another metal, such as gold

aqua regia mixture of concentrated nitric acid and hydrochloric acid that can dissolve gold and platinum

artificial man-made

atom smallest particle of an element that has the properties of that element. Atoms contain smaller particles called sub-atomic particles.

atomic number number of protons in the nucleus of an atom. It is also called the proton number.

bond force that join atoms together

brittle word that describes a solid that breaks into small pieces when hit. Glass is a brittle solid because it breaks into small pieces when hit with a hammer.

bullion bars of precious metal, especially gold or silver

carat (karat in the USA) a measure of the purity of gold. One carat is 1/24th or 4.17 per cent, so 12 carat gold is 50 per cent gold.

catalyst substance that speeds up a reaction without getting used up

cathode negatively charged electrode

ceramic tough solid made by heating clay and other substances to high temperatures in an oven. Plates, bathroom tiles and toilet bowls are made from ceramics.

compound substance made from the atoms of two or more elements, joined together by chemical bonds.

corrosion when a substance forms on the surface of a metal. Usually this is an oxide of the metal produced when the metal reacts with oxygen in the air.

decay when the nucleus of a radioactive substance breaks up, giving off radiation and becoming the nucleus of another element, it decays

decompose when a compound breaks down into simpler substances, such as the elements in them. For example, water can decompose to make hydrogen and oxygen.

density mass of a substance compared to its volume. Substances with a high density feel very heavy for their size.

ductile easily pulled into a thin wire

electrode solid that conducts electricity, such as graphite or a metal. Electrodes are found in batteries and are also used in electrolysis and electroplating.

electrolysis breaking down or decomposing a compound by passing electricity through it. The compound must be molten or dissolved in a liquid for electrolysis to work.

electron sub-atomic particle with a negative electric charge, found around the nucleus of an atom

electroplating coating a metal with another metal using electricity

element substance made from one type of atom. Elements cannot be broken down into simpler substances.

extract to remove a chemical from a mixture of chemicals

fungicide chemical that kills fungi and moulds

group vertical column of elements in the periodic table. Elements in a group have similar properties.

ion charged particle made when an atom loses or gains electrons. If a metal atom loses electrons it becomes a positive ion. If a non-metal atom gains electrons it becomes a negative ion.

isotope isotopes are atoms of an element with the same number of protons and electrons, but different numbers of neutrons. They share the same atomic number but they have a different mass number.

malleable the word that describes a solid that can be bent into shape without breaking

mass number in the nucleus of an atom, the number of protons added to the number of neutrons

mineral substance that is found naturally but does not come from animals or plants. Metal ores and limestone are examples of minerals.

molecule smallest particle of an element or compound that exists by itself. A molecule is usually made from two or more atoms joined together.

mordant chemical that helps a dye to stick to fabric fibres

native found as the pure metallic element, not combined in a compound

neutron sub-atomic particle with no electric charge, found in the nucleus of an atom

nucleus part of an atom made from protons and neutrons. It has a positive electric charge and is found at the centre of the atom.

ore mineral from which metals can be taken out and purified

period horizontal row of elements in the periodic table

periodic table table in which all the known elements are arranged into groups and periods

phosphor chemical that gives off light when it absorbs energy

pigment solid substance that gives colour to a paint. Pigments do not dissolve in water.

precipitate solid that appears when two solutions are mixed

product substance made in a chemical reaction

proton sub-atomic particle with a positive electric charge, found in the nucleus of an atom

proton number number of protons in the nucleus of an atom. It is also called the atomic number. No two elements have the same proton number.

radioactive substance that can produce radiation

radiation energy or particles given off when an atom decays

reaction chemical change that produces new substances

reduce to take away oxygen from an element or compound in a chemical reaction. For example, iron oxide is reduced to iron when it reacts with carbon.

refining removing impurities from a substance to make it more pure. It can also mean separating the different substances in a mixture, for example, in oil refining.

sacrificial protection method used to stop iron and steel rusting using a more reactive metal such as cadmium or zinc

sub-atomic particle particle smaller than an atom, such as proton, neutron and electron

tracer chemical, often radioactive, that scientists can easily follow to see where it goes

ultraviolet light high-energy light which is invisible to us

volatile when a substance turns into a gas easily

weld join between two pieces of metals, usually made by heating them

Timeline

copper, gold, iron, mercury and silver discovered	ancient times	
cobalt discovered	1735	Georg Brandt
platinum discovered	1735	Antonio de Ulloa
first commercial European production of zinc	1743	William Champion
nickel discovered	1751	Axel Cronstedt
osmium discovered	1803	Smithson Tennant
palladium and rhodium discovered	1803	William Wollaston
iridium discovered	1804	Smithson Tennant
platinum isolated in a workable form	1805	William Wollaston
cadmium discovered	1817	Friedrich Stromeyer
ruthenium discovered	1828	Gottfried Osann
meitnerium, hassium, ununnilium and ununbium first made	1982–1996	Institute for Heavy Ion Research, Germany

Further reading and useful websites

Books

Fullick, Ann, *Science Topics: Chemicals in Action* (Heinemann Library, 1999)

Knapp, Brian, *The Elements* series, particularly *Copper, Silver and Gold*; *Zinc, Cadmium and Mercury* (Atlantic Europe Publishing Co, 1996)

Oxlade, Chris, *Chemicals in Action* series, particularly *Metals*; *Atoms*; *Elements and Compounds* (Heinemann Library, 2002)

Websites

WebElements™
http://www.webelements.com
An interactive periodic table crammed with information and photographs.

DiscoverySchool
http://school.discovery.com/students
Help for science projects and homework, and free science clip art.

Proton Don
http://www.funbrain.com/periodic
The fun periodic table quiz!

BBC Science
http://www.bbc.co.uk/science
Quizzes, news, information and games about all areas of science.

Creative Chemistry
http://www.creative-chemistry.org.uk
An interactive chemistry site with fun practical activities, quizzes, puzzles and more.

Mineralology Database
http://www.webmineral.com
Lots of useful information about minerals, including colour photographs and information about their chemistry.

Index

Titles in the *Periodic Table* series include:

Hardback   0 431 16981 0

Hardback   0 431 16982 9

Hardback   0 431 16984 5

Hardback   0 431 16983 7

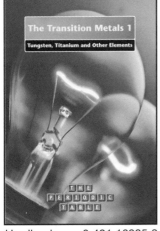

Hardback   0 431 16985 3

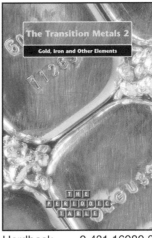

Hardback   0 431 16980 2

Find out about the other titles in this series on our website www.heinemann.co.uk/library